Collins MUSIC

GET SET! PIANO
Christmas Crackers

Karen Marshall · David Blackwell

Illustrated by Julia Patton

CW00953354

CONTENTS

*Includes version for more advanced pupils

Good King Wenceslas

- Can you tap the pulse as your teacher plays this carol?

Words: J.M. Neale
Melody: from *Piae Cantiones*
arr. KM

With a confident stride

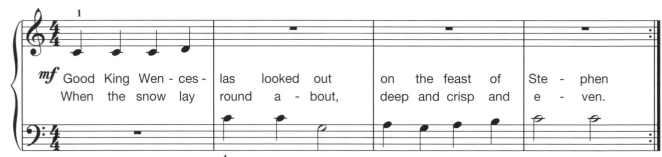

mf Good King Wen - ces - las looked out on the feast of Ste - phen
When the snow lay round a - bout, deep and crisp and e - ven.

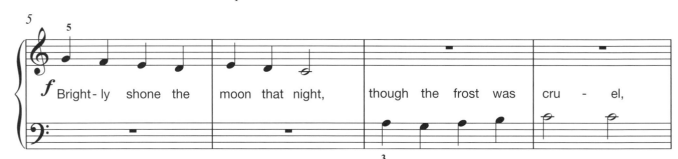

f Bright - ly shone the moon that night, though the frost was cru - el,

When a poor man came in sight gath-'ring win - ter fu - el.

Duet part

arr. DB

With a confident stride

Practice

Wenceslas was a ruler in what is now the Czech Republic in the early tenth century. This picture of him has 13 sections for you to colour, one for each bar of music. Colour it in when you have learnt that bar.

Jolly old Saint Nicholas

Words: E. Miller
Music: J.R. Murray
arr. KM

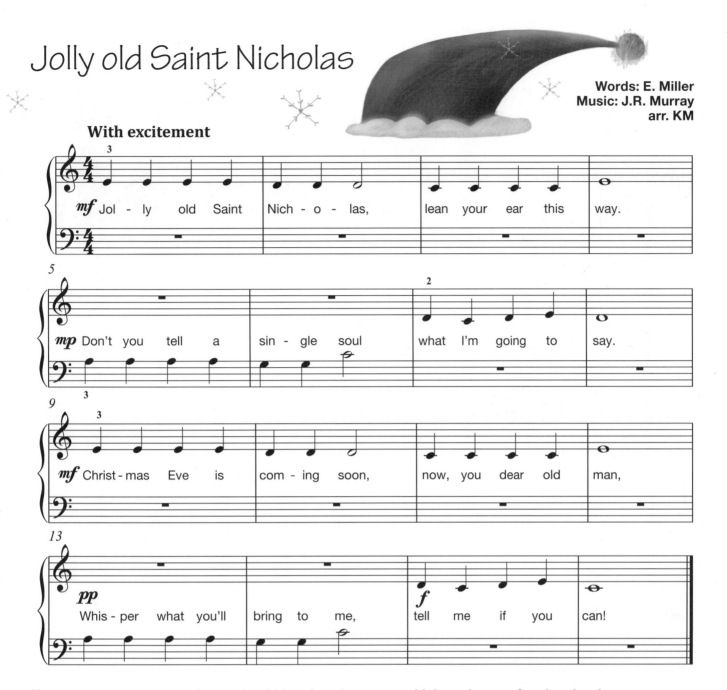

With excitement

mf Jol - ly old Saint Nich - o - las, lean your ear this way.

mp Don't you tell a sin - gle soul what I'm going to say.

mf Christ - mas Eve is com - ing soon, now, you dear old man,

pp Whis - per what you'll bring to me, f tell me if you can!

Note to teacher: the pupil part should be played an octave higher when performing the duet.

Duet part

arr. DB

Fun fact

Saint Nicholas was a bishop of the early church who gave gifts to the poor. The idea of Father Christmas is based on Saint Nicholas. In some European countries, children leave out shoes on Saint Nicholas' Day on 6 December to be filled with sweets and presents.

O come, all ye faithful

- Identify all the dynamics in the music and write the meaning in the boxes provided.

Words and Music: J.F. Wade
arr. KM

mf means _____

f means _____

mp means _____

Note to teacher: the pupil part should be played an octave higher when performing the duet.

Duet part

arr. DB

Note to teacher: the melody and right hand of the duet part can be played with the alternative rhythm given below the stave in bars 7 and 19.

Up on the housetop

- Can you tap the heart-beat pulse while your teacher plays this piece?
- Draw a circle around the *staccato* notes – make sure you play them lightly and crisply.

Fun fact
This song was written in 1864 by Benjamin Hanby. It is believed to be one of the first songs to mention Father Christmas.

B. Hanby
arr. KM

Note to teacher: the pupil part should be played an octave higher when performing the duet.

Duet part

arr. DB

Note to teacher: the first two bars of the duet part can be played as an introduction.

Jingle, bells

Version 1 *(advanced student / duet part)*

J. Pierpont
arr. DB

Note to teacher: this version of 'Jingle, bells' is for more advanced pupils. It can be played as a duet with version 2.

Version 2

- You can play 'Jingle, bells' as a duet with version 1 by playing two octaves higher. Find a bell and play this on each crotchet beat in the verse, then join in with the chorus. Find your starting note before you play!

J. Pierpont
arr. KM

Happily

Fun fact

'Jingle, bells' was the first song broadcast from space. In December 1965, the astronauts of Gemini 6 pretended to Mission Control that they could see Father Christmas on his sleigh. They played 'Jingle, bells' on sleigh bells and a tiny harmonica that they had smuggled on board!

Practice

- Write in the number of beats by each of the notes in your part: $\frac{1}{2}$, 1, 2 or 4.

Away in a manger

- Can you make this sound really *legato* (smooth)? What sign on the music tells you to do this?

W.J. Kirkpatrick
arr. KM and DB

Note to teacher: the pupil part should be played an octave higher when performing the duet.

Duet part

arr. DB

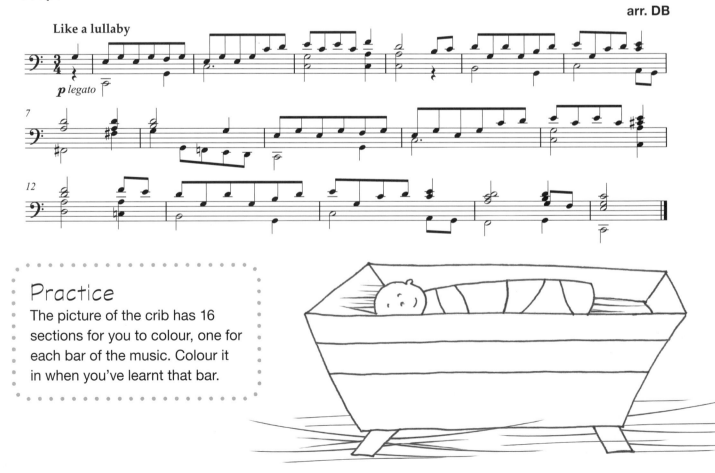

Practice

The picture of the crib has 16 sections for you to colour, one for each bar of the music. Colour it in when you've learnt that bar.

Infant holy, infant lowly

- Can you name the left-hand notes at the end of this piece?

Words: translated by E.M. Reed
Music: Polish traditional
arr. KM

Notes: __ __ __ __ __ __ __

Note to teacher: the pupil part should be played an octave higher when performing the duet.

Duet part

arr. DB

9

MUSICAL CRACKERS 1: Sharps and flats

Can you remember what sharps and flats are? Fill in the sentences below.

A sharp (♯) means you play the note a semitone _h_ __ __ __ __ __

A flat (♭) means you play the note a semitone _l_ __ __ __ __

Colour in the cracker ends when you've completed each exercise.

- Try playing this Christmas cracker joke. Notice all the sharp signs!

What's the name of San-ta's dog? San-ta Paws!

- Now here's a joke for left hand. Look out for the flats in this one.

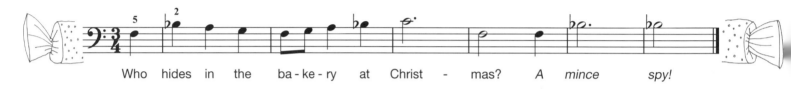

Who hides in the ba-ke-ry at Christ-mas? A mince spy!

How many B flats are there? _____

- A sharp or flat sign affects all the other notes on the same line or space for the rest of the bar.
  Play this cracker joke for both hands:

What do mon-keys sing at Christ-mas? Jun-gle bells, Jun-gle bells!

Did you play all the F sharps? How many are there? _____

- The **key signature** appears at the beginning of a piece of music and shows you which sharps or flats you need to play.

- All the Bs in this cracker joke will be B flat. Can you play it correctly?

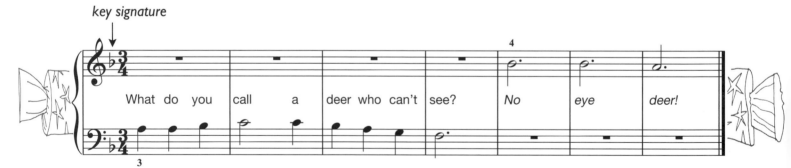

What do you call a deer who can't see? No eye deer!

Look out for key signatures in the next carols.

Snowflakes

Here's a Christmas piece for you to make up yourself using the black notes on the piano.

The black notes on the piano can be written as sharps or flats:

- Play these on the piano in different octaves, using either the left or the right hand.
- Now make up a tune using these notes while your teacher plays the duet part below. Play them in any order and in any rhythm – find a tune you like.
- Think about snowflakes and how you can suggest them in your tune. They are soft and delicate and float gently in the air, so maybe your tune will also be soft and the notes will move gently around the keyboard.
- Enjoy making up your tune!

Duet part

DB

Note to teacher: this could be played through once as an introduction.

11

Under Bethl'hem's star so bright

Czech traditional
arr. KM

Simply

mp Un - der Beth - l'hem's star so bright, Shep - herds watched their flocks by night.

mf Hy - dom, hy - dom, tid - li - dom, Hy - dom, hy - dom, tid - li - dom.

The holly and the ivy

- Clap the pulse as your teacher plays this, stressing the first beat of each three in a bar.

English traditional
arr. KM and DB

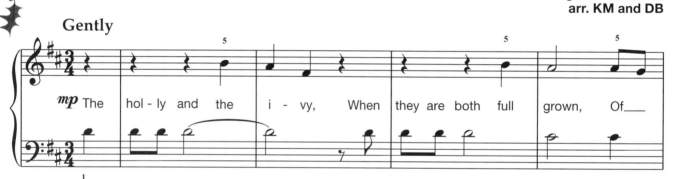

Gently

mp The hol - ly and the i - vy, When they are both full grown, Of___

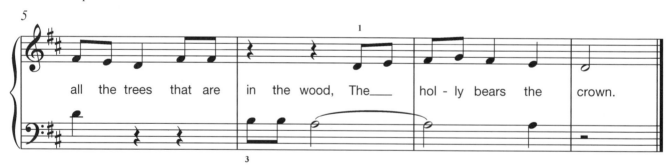

all the trees that are in the wood, The___ hol - ly bears the crown.

Fun fact
The bright red berries of the holly and the shiny green leaves of the ivy brighten the winter garden and stand for the new life of the baby Jesus.

Practice
This picture of some holly has eight sections for you to colour, one for each bar of the music. Colour it in when you've learnt that bar.

The first Nowell

- Can you spot the dotted crotchets in this carol? Draw a circle round each one.
- Clap the rhythm of bar 1, counting six quavers while you do this. Your teacher can help you.

English traditional
arr. DB

The__ first_____ No - well the__ an - gel did say Was to

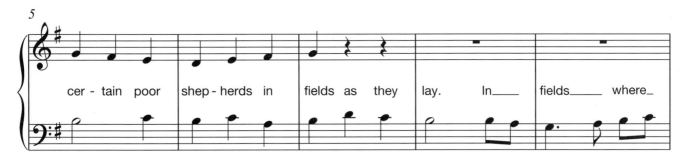

cer - tain poor shep - herds in fields as they lay. In_____ fields_____ where_

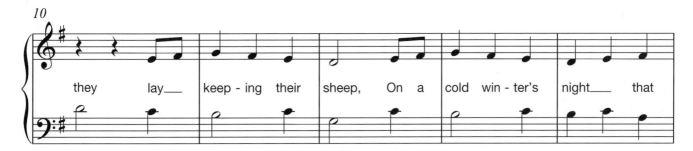

they lay__ keep - ing their sheep, On a cold win - ter's night_____ that

was_____ so deep. *f* No - well,_____ No - well, No - well, No -

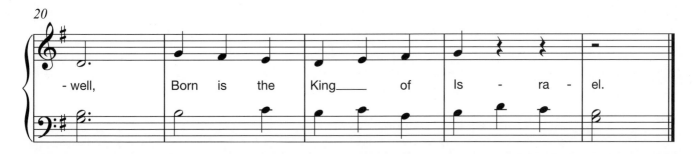

- well, Born is the King_____ of Is - ra - el.

Fun fact
Christmas was banned in England in the middle of the 17th century, but people continued to sing carols in secret.

O little town of Bethlehem

- This carol uses the right sustain pedal, which makes notes last longer. Use the ball of your foot to move the pedal, keeping your heel on the floor.
- Try playing this piece an octave higher to make it sound more sparkling.

Words: P. Brooks
Music: English traditional
arr. KM

14

We wish you a Merry Christmas

- Can you clap the pulse while your teacher plays your part,
  making the first beat of each bar a louder clap?

English traditional
arr. DB

Happily

mf We | wish you a mer - ry | Christ - mas, We | wish you a mer - ry | Christ - mas, We

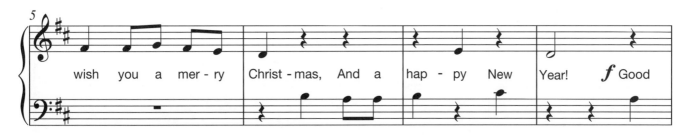

wish you a mer - ry | Christ - mas, And a | hap - py New | Year! *f* Good

tid - ings we | bring To | you and your | kin; We

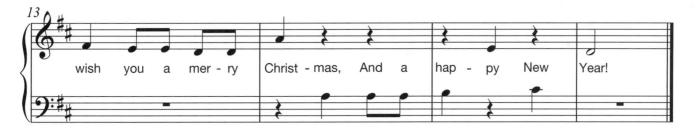

wish you a mer - ry | Christ - mas, And a | hap - py New | Year!

Note to teacher: the pupil part should be played an octave higher when performing the duet.

Duet part

arr. DB

Happily

mf

f

Fun fact

This carol from the west of England was sung in olden times by carol-singers going from door to door at Christmas and singing carols in return for food and drink. The second verse begins, 'Now bring us some figgy pudding' – something very like our Christmas pudding.

Once in royal David's city

Words: C.F. Alexander
Music: H.J. Gauntlett
arr. KM

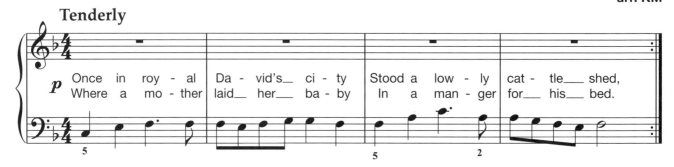

Once in roy - al Da - vid's_ ci - ty Stood a low - ly cat - tle_ shed,
Where a mo - ther laid_ her_ ba - by In a man - ger for_ his_ bed.

Ma - ry was that mo - ther mild, Je - sus Christ her lit - tle_ child.

Note to teacher: the pupil part should be played an octave higher when performing the duet.

Duet part

arr. DB

Practice

The picture of a cattle shed has eight sections for you to colour, one for each bar of the music.
Colour it in when you've learnt that bar.

Hark! The herald angels sing

- Can you spot the C major scale? Practise this before you play the piece.
- Can you locate the dotted notes? Clap the rhythm of bar 3, counting in quavers. (Hint: there are eight quavers to count!)

Words: C. Wesley
Music: F. Mendelssohn
arr. KM

Silent night

- Look out for the dotted crotchets. Put a star by all the bars containing dotted crotchets to make sure you play them correctly.

F. Gruber
arr. DB

Duet part

arr. DB

Deck the hall

- There are lots of dotted crotchets in this carol. It's helpful to count quavers in the bars where these appear.

Welsh traditional
arr. KM

Happily

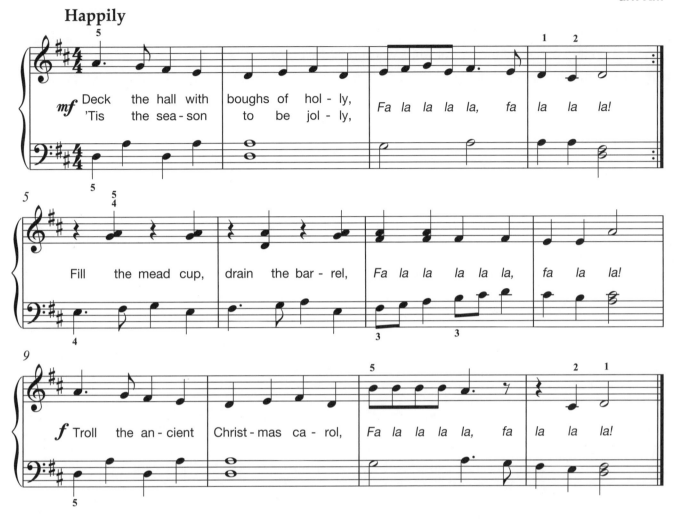

Deck the hall with boughs of hol - ly,
'Tis the sea - son to be jol - ly,
Fa la la la la, fa la la la!

Fill the mead cup, drain the bar - rel, Fa la la la la la, fa la la!

Troll the an - cient Christ - mas ca - rol, Fa la la la la, fa la la la!

Fun fact
This Welsh dance-carol was originally performed on New Year's Eve. The famous composer Joseph Haydn arranged it for singer and piano, with optional parts for violin and cello.

Practice
This picture has 12 sections for you to colour, one for each bar of music. Colour it in when you have learnt that bar.

The Virgin Mary had a baby boy

'The Virgin Mary had a baby boy' has **syncopated rhythms**. This means that some of the notes are placed just before or just after the beat, creating a bit of a surprise.

- Listen to your teacher play your part through. Can you sing or say the words in rhythm as the music is played?
- Now try singing or saying the words while walking to the pulse.
- Finally, tap the rhythm duet below on the lid of the piano or table top with your right and left hands. This is the music from the end of bar 2 to bar 6.

Now you're ready to have a go at playing your part!

Duet part

arr. DB

20

Caribbean traditional
arr. DB

MUSICAL CRACKERS 2:
Note reading and musical terms

Each cracker includes a melody from a well-known Christmas carol. Colour in the cracker ends when you have played the melody and filled in all the missing note names and words.

Rocking carol

- Fill in the boxes with the note names.

Czech traditional

Coventry carol

- Fill in the boxes with the note names and answer the two questions.

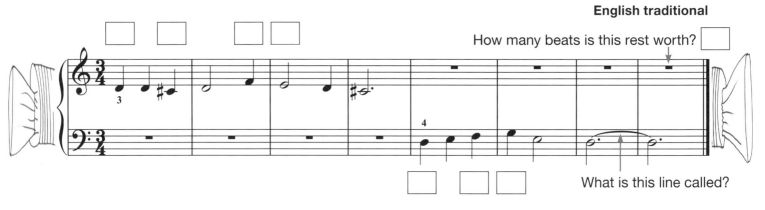

English traditional

How many beats is this rest worth? ☐

What is this line called?

_____

O Christmas tree

- Choose a tempo mark for this carol and add it in the box at the start. Can you write in the meaning of each of these tempo marks?

Moderato: _____   Andante: _____   Allegro: _____

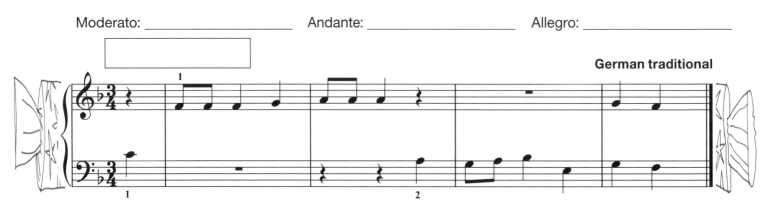

German traditional

- What is the key signature? _____

  Circle the one note that is affected by the key signature.

The cherry tree carol

Before you play this carol, clap the rhythm and say the note names out loud.

Now add some dynamics. Choose from the following and describe them in the space provided:

f: _____   *p*: _____   *crescendo*: _____

mf: _____   *mp*: _____

English traditional

- What is the key of this piece? _____
- What does the time signature mean? _____

Il est né

The title of this French carol means 'He is born'. Before you play it, clap the rhythm and say the note names out loud. Can you spot the dynamics? Be ready to play them correctly!

- Add the correct time signature at the start.
- What is the key of this carol? _____

French traditional

Ding dong! merrily on high

Version 1 *(advanced student / duet part)*

Words: G.R. Woodward
Music: T. Arbeau
arr. DB

Gloria, Hosanna in excelsis!: Glory, Hosanna in the highest! (Hosanna: a shout of praise)

Note to teacher: this version is for more advanced pupils. It can be played as a duet with version 2.

Fun fact

The words of this carol were written by George Woodward, who played the euphonium and who enjoyed bell-ringing!

Version 2

- Fill in the boxes above the notes with the correct note names.

Words: G.R. Woodward
Music: T. Arbeau
arr. KM

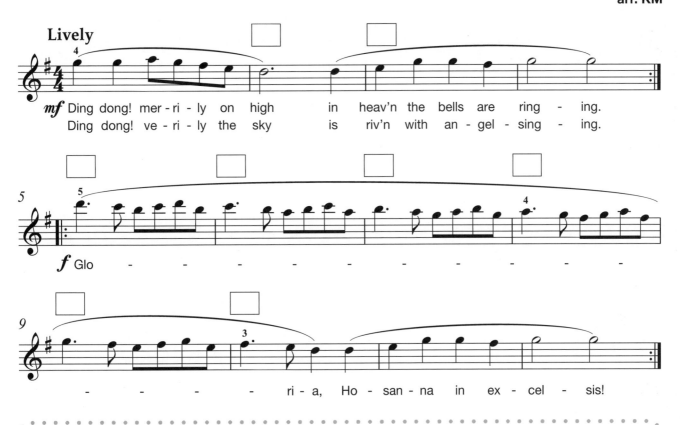

Lively

mf Ding dong! mer - ri - ly on high in heav'n the bells are ring - ing.
Ding dong! ve - ri - ly the sky is riv'n with an - gel - sing - ing.

f Glo - - - - - ri - a, Ho - san - na in ex - cel - sis!

....

Practice

The bells have 12 sections for you to colour. Each one represents a bar of the music. Colour it in when you have learnt that bar.

....

God rest you merry, gentlemen

Version 1

- Fill in the boxes above the notes with the correct note names.

English traditional
arr. KM

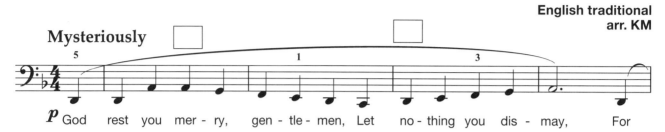

Mysteriously

p God rest you mer - ry, gen - tle - men, Let no - thing you dis - may, For

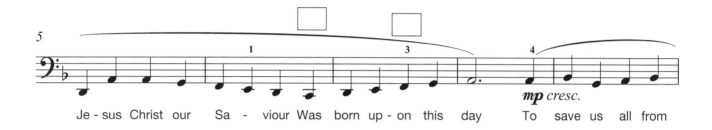

Je - sus Christ our Sa - viour Was born up - on this day To save us all from

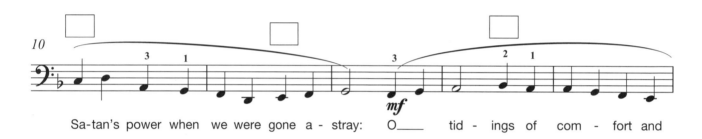

Sa-tan's power when we were gone a - stray: O___ tid - ings of com - fort and

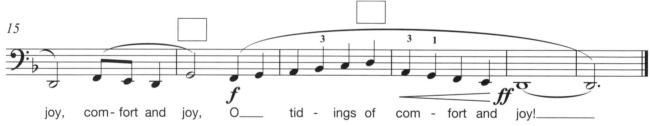

joy, com - fort and joy, O___ tid - ings of com - fort and joy!___

Practice

The picture of the festive gentlemen has 20 sections for you to colour, one for each bar of the music. Colour it in when you have learnt that bar.

Fun fact

In his famous book *A Christmas Carol* from 1843, Charles Dickens has a carol singer try to sing this carol to grumpy Ebenezer Scrooge. The word 'merry' means happy and joyous.

Version 2 *(advanced student / duet part)*

English traditional
arr. DB

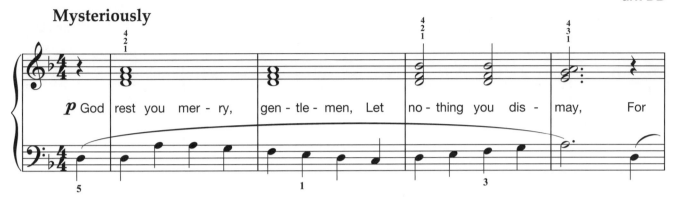

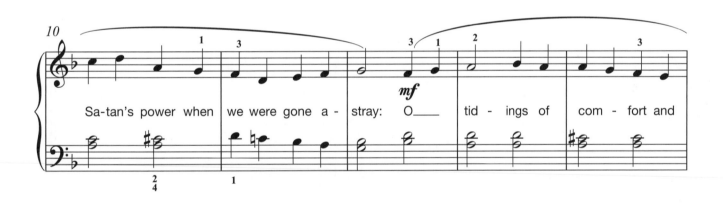

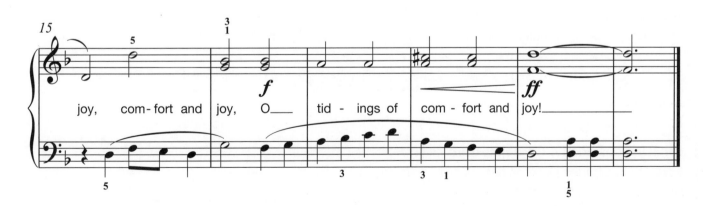

Note to teacher: this version is for more advanced pupils. It can be played as a duet with version 1.

Huron carol

- Play the scale of G natural minor before you play this piece: G A B♭ C D E♭ F G.

Canadian traditional
arr. DB

With a sense of wonder

'Twas in the moon of win-ter-time when all the birds had fled, That might-y Git-chi Man-i-tou* sent an-gel choirs in-stead. Be-fore their light the stars grew dim, and wan-d'ring hun-ters heard the hymn: Je-sus, your king, is born, Je-sus is born, In ex-cel-sis glo-ri-a!** In excelsis gloria!

*Gitchi Manitou: Great Spirit (God)   ** In excelsis gloria!: Glory in the highest!

Duet part

arr. DB

With a sense of wonder

28

Patapan

- Clap these rhythms before you play:

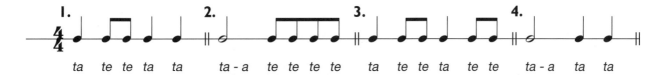

1.	2.	3.	4.
ta te te ta ta	ta - a te te te te	ta te te ta te te	ta - a ta ta

- Can you spot where these rhythms appear in the music?
- This carol is from France, and underneath the rhythms we've added the French time names. Try saying these names aloud in rhythm.

French traditional, words adap. arr. KM

- There are lots of different dynamics in this piece. Try shading in the bars with different colours to represent the different dynamics – red for **ff**, blue for **p**, etc.

The bells of Christmas

- Play both hands an octave higher in this piece to sound like Christmas bells, and hold the pedal down throughout. What carol do you play in your left hand in the last line?

DB

With a ringing sound!

hold the pedal down throughout

Carol: _____

More Christmas bells

- Here are some Christmas bells for you to play in different keys.

- Can you play the bells in F major? Here's the start!

MUSICAL CRACKERS 3:
Compound time signatures

Compound time signatures are time signatures that can be divided by three. Some of the carols in the rest of this book use them.

$\frac{6}{8}$ = 6 quavers in a bar. This can also be divided by three to make two beats.

$\frac{9}{8}$ = 9 quavers in a bar. This can also be divided by three to make three beats.

$\frac{12}{8}$ = 12 quavers in a bar. This can also be divided by three to make four beats.

Colour in the cracker ends or mini crackers when you've completed each exercise or piece.

- Clap the rhythms below, then circle the notes and rest into dotted crotchet units.

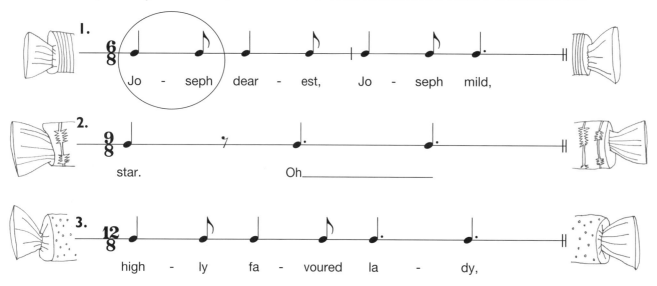

Joseph dearest, Joseph mild

- This carol uses the compound time signature $\frac{6}{8}$.

German, 15th century
arr. KM

32

Gabriel's message

- Clap the rhythm of the right hand, noticing that the time signature changes between $\frac{9}{8}$ and $\frac{12}{8}$.

Basque carol
arr. DB

Gently

mp The an-gel Ga-bri-el from | hea-ven came, His | wings as drift-ed snow, his

eyes____ as flame. *mf* 'All | hail,' said he, 'thou low-ly maid-en Ma | ry, Most

high-ly fa-voured la | dy,' Glo — — ri-a!

Christmas is coming

- This short piece is a **round**, which means two people can play together, starting at different times.
  Try playing this with your teacher, friend or relative, using different octaves on the piano.
  The second player can begin after two beats or at the start of bar 2 (at the places marked *).

DB

Christ-mas is com-ing, the geese are get-ting fat. Please put a pen-ny in the old man's hat.

Cantemos a María

- Some of the notes in this carol can be **syncopated** – do you remember what this means? Try syncopating the right-hand notes where indicated in the music:

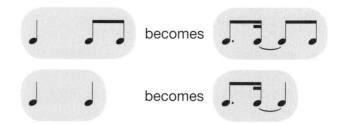

- Look out for the semiquavers at the beginning and end of this piece – there are four of these in one crotchet. Try saying the French rhythm names: bar 1 is '*ti ka ti ka te*'.

Dominican Republic traditional
arr. DB

While shepherds watched their flocks

Words: N. Tate
Music: Este's Psalter
arr. DB

- Can you play the tune (right hand) a tone higher, in G major? Here are the first two notes:

- Try playing it in G an octave higher with this accompaniment. Listen to the opening and start playing the tune at the end of bar 4.

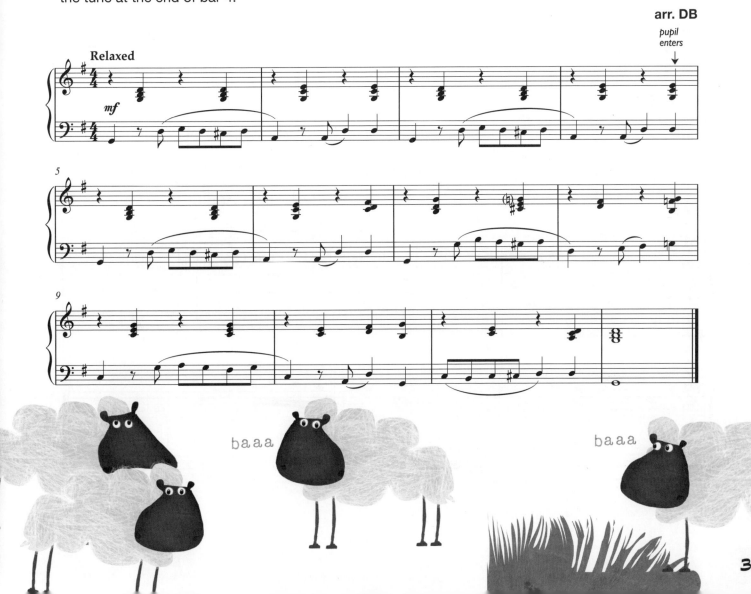

Mary rocked her baby!

- This piece is a challenge! Practise all the jumps around the piano silently, without playing the notes.
- Look out for the repeated passages.

American spiritual
arr. DB

I saw three ships

- Can you clap the pulse while your teacher plays this carol to you? Remember: it's two dotted crotchet beats in a bar.
- Can you spot the little note before the chords in the left hand? This is an **ornament** or 'crushed' note. Your teacher will help you play this.

**English traditional
arr. KM and DB**

Fun fact

No one quite knows what the three ships in this folk carol mean, but they could refer to the camels used by the three kings who brought gifts to Jesus, as camels are known as 'ships of the desert'.

Practice

These three ships have 12 sections for you to colour, one for each bar of the music. Colour it in when you have learnt that bar.

Y Gelynnen (The Holly)

- Can you see in bar 3 there are *staccato* notes in the right hand and *legato* ones in the left? You can practise this silently on the lid of the piano before you play. Try to feel the difference between *legato* in one hand and *staccato* in the other.

Welsh traditional
arr. DB

We three kings of Orient are

• Can you spot where the music changes time signature?

J.H. Hopkins
arr. DB

At a steady pace

mp We three kings of Or - i - ent are, Bear - ing gifts we tra-verse a - far.

Field and foun - tain, moor and moun - tain, Fol - low-ing yon - der star. Oh____

f Star of won - der, star of night, Star with roy - al beau - ty bright,

West - ward lead - ing, still pro-ceed - ing, Guide us to thy per - fect light.

Practice
This picture of the three kings has 16 sections, one for each bar of the music. Colour it in when you have learnt that bar.

Go, tell it on the mountain

- Check out how to play this piece before you start. The **D.C. al Coda** at bar 16 means go back to the beginning and play through to finish with the Coda. When you reach the end of bar 6 for the second time, jump down to the Coda at the bottom of the page.

African American spiritual
arr. DB